Events of

News for every day of the year

The last Triumph TR7 sports car, produced by British Leyland in October 1981.

By Hugh Morrison

MONTPELIER PUBLISHING

Front cover (clockwise from left): The robot Canadarm on use aboard the Space Shuttle. Stamp commemorating the Royal Wedding of Prince Charles and Lady Diana. Wimbledon champion John McEnroe. The IBM Personal Computer with MS-DOS.

Back cover (clockwise from top): The Rolling Stones on their 1981 US tour. Logo for MTV. Saturn photographed by the *Voyager* space probe. *Donkey Kong* arcade game. The attempted assassination of Ronald Reagan. President Reagan. The Triumph Acclaim.

Image credits: Milborne One, Prince Power, Charles 01, Dysepsion, Gage Skidmore, Eva Rinaldi, Allen Warren, Anefo, Teddy Van Pelt, Gil Zetbase, Mike Cattell, Rob Bogaerts/Anefo, Imk3nnyma, Jean-Louise Debaize, Michael Evans, LSE Library, Bilby, Kim Aldis, Stefan Woclaw, Keith Ballard/USAF, Jonathan Andel, Phillippe Roos, Rob Croes/Anefo, David Hume Kennerly, Yuri Somyov, Ian Visits, Studio Harcourt, Chris Evert, Joshua Driggs, Noemi Nunez, Tony Harp, RP Fitzgerald, Dr Lee Lowery, Fernando Pereira/Anefo, Rouse Rouse, Federigo Federighi, Esther Lim, NASA, Morio, Charles 01, National Archives/Africa Through a Lens, Claudio Mariotto, Rob Bogaerts/Anefo, Rod Hull, Herbert Behrens/Anefo, University of Michigan, Vauxford, Marcel Antonisse/Anefo, Patricia Fitzgerald, Charles 01, Allan Warren, Israeli Defence Force, NASA, Archives New Zealand, Carl Van Vechten, Glenn Francis, Les Golding, J Żołnierkiewicz, Motown Records.

This edition © Montpelier Publishing 2020. All rights reserved.
ISBN: 9798685175342

January 1981

Thursday 1: Greece joins the Common Market (now the European Union).

The US minimum wage increases from $3.10 to $3.35 per hour.

Friday 2: The serial killer Peter Sutcliffe, (the 'Yorkshire Ripper'), is finally caught after a six year manhunt in the north of England.

Saturday 3: HRH Princess Alice, the last surviving grandchild of Queen Victoria, dies aged 97.

Sunday 4: The most expensive Broadway play to this date, *Frankenstein* by Victor Gialanella opens and closes the same day due to poor reviews.

Monday 5: The popular sci-fi comedy series *The Hitchhiker's Guide to the Galaxy* by Douglas Adams is first broadcast on BBC TV.

Left: HRH Princess Alice.

January 1981

Ronald Reagan.

Tuesday 6: The results of the US Electoral College are announced: Ronald Reagan is officially certified as having won the 1979 US Presidential election.

Wednesday 7: The New York Stock Exchange has the biggest trading day in its history to this date, after respected analyst Joe Granville sends a two word message to his investors: 'sell everything'.

Thursday 8: Renato Nicolai, 55, claims to have seen a flying saucer above his farm in Trans-en-Provence, France. French government scientists investigate and find unusual burn marks and metal deposits at the site.

Friday 9: The funeral of HRH Princess Alice takes place at St George's Chapel, Windsor.

Saturday 10: The 11 year long guerilla war by Marxist rebels in El Salvador begins.

Sunday 11: The Iranian government accepts the return of $11bn of seized Iranian assets as a ransom for the release of 52 US hostages.

Joan Collins.

Monday 12: The TV series *Dynasty* starring Joan Collins begins its nine year run on NBC.

Tuesday 13: Donna Griffiths, 12, of Pershore, Worcestershire, England, begins 978 days of repetitive sneezing twice a minute.

January 1981

Wednesday 14: The first extended-wear contact lenses are approved for sale in the USA.

Thursday 15: The ground-breaking US police drama series *Hill Street Blues* is first broadcast on NBC-TV.

Friday 16: Northern Irish nationalist MP Bernadette Devlin McAliskey survives being shot nine times in an assassination attempt by Loyalist paramilitaries near Coalisland, County Tyrone.

Saturday 17: President Ferdinand Marcos of the Philippines declares an end to eight years of martial law.

Sunday 18: Thirteen black youngsters die in a house fire in New Cross Road, London SE14; the cause is never identified but arson by a far-right group is alleged.

Monday 19: The Iran hostage crisis officially ends when the Algiers Accord is signed between the USA and Iran.

Tuesday 20: Ronald Reagan is sworn into office as the 40th President of the United States.

Wednesday 21: The first DeLorean sports car is manufactured in Dunmurry, Northern Ireland.

The DeLorean: the car later achieves fame in the 1985 film *Back to the Future*.

January 1981

Thursday 22: The East German football stars Gerd Weber, Matthias Müller and Peter Kotte are arrested by the secret police on charges of attempted defection to the west.

Friday 23: US composer Samuel Barber, best known for his *Adagio for Strings* (1936) dies aged 70.

Saturday 24: 150 people are killed in a 6.8 magnitude earthquake in Sichuan, China.

Sunday 25: A group of former Labour Party cabinet members known as the 'Gang of Four' announce the formation of Britain's new Social Democratic Party (SDP).

The actor Elijah Wood is born on 28 January.

The singer Alicia Keys is born in New York City.

Monday 26: The US Supreme Court rules in Chandler *v* Florida that the televising of court proceedings is lawful.

Tuesday 27: 471 people are killed when the Indonesian ferry *Tampomas II* sinks in the Java Sea.

Wednesday 28: All US Federal price controls on fuel, in place since 1971, are lifted.

The actor Elijah Wood (*Lord of the Rings*) is born in Cedar Rapids, Iowa.

The singer Alicia Keys is born on 25 January.

January 1981

Justin Timberlake is born on 31 January.

Thursday 29: It is announced that the Japanese car firm Nissan will manufacture Datsun cars in the UK.

Friday 30: South African commandos carry out a border raid against African National Congress bases in Mozambique.

Saturday 31: The first parade for veterans of the Vietnam War is held in Indianapolis, Indiana, eight years after the end of US involvement in the conflict.

The singer Justin Timberlake is born in Memphis, Tennessee.

February 1981

Sunday 1: Australia defeats New Zealand in the Cricket World Cup by bowling underarm; although legal the practice is considered unsporting and is banned.

Monday 2: Golfer John Cook wins the Bing Crosby National Pro-Am tournament in California after winning an extra hole following a five-way tie.

Tuesday 3: Dr Gro Harlem Bruntland becomes the first woman prime minister of Norway.

Wednesday 4: Britain's prime minister Margaret Thatcher announces the government will sell half its shares in British Aerospace.

Thursday 5: The actor Lord (Laurence) Olivier receives the Order of Merit in the Queen's New Year's Honours List.

Friday 6: HRH The Prince of Wales proposes marriage to Lady Diana Spencer.

Left: Lord Olivier, who receives the Order of Merit on 5 February.

February 1981

Saturday 7: 24 senior Soviet military personnel, including the Admiral of the Pacific Fleet, are killed in a plane crash near Leningrad.

Sunday 8: The worst tragedy in Greek sporting history takes place when 24 people are killed in a stampede during a football match in Piraeus near Athens.

Monday 9: The singer Bill Haley, generally considered to have recorded the first rock and roll song (*Rock Around the Clock*) in 1954, dies aged 55.

The rock and roll pioneer Bill Haley dies on 9 February.

Tuesday 10: Eight people die in a major fire in the Las Vegas Hilton hotel.

Wednesday 11: The closure of Britain's Talbot motor plant at Linwood, Renfrewshire, is announced.

Thursday 12: The discovery of a previously unknown symphony by Mozart, *Symphony in F Major* (1765), is announced.

Canadian rock band Rush release their album *Moving Pictures*.

Friday 13: *The Times* newspaper of London is bought by the Australian press baron Rupert Murdoch.

Saturday 14: 49 people are killed in a fire at the Stardust Cabaret disco in Dublin, Ireland.

Sunday 15: Richard Petty wins the Daytona 500 NASCAR motor race.

NASCAR champion Richard Petty.

The first Sunday games take place in England's Football League.

February 1981

Monday 16: A would-be assassin accidentally blows himself up just before Pope John Paul II celebrates mass in Karachi, Pakistan, with a congregation of 70,000.

Tuesday 17: The socialite and Hilton Hotels heiress Paris Hilton is born in New York City.

HRH Princess Anne is elected Chancellor of London University.

Wednesday 18: US President Ronald Reagan introduces a package of reforms to reduce inflation and unemployment.

Thursday 19: The singer Frank Sinatra is cleared of rumoured links to organised crime, and his casino operating licence, revoked in 1963, is restored.

Paris Hilton is born on 17 February.

Friday 20: An Argentinian Airlines plane narrowly avoids hitting the top of New York City's World Trade Center in thick fog.

Saturday 21: In Manila in the Phillippines, Pope John Paul II calls for a series of inter-faith meetings with the world's religious leaders.

Sunday 22: The veteran vaudeville comedian Joe Smith (of Smith and Dale) dies aged 97.

Monday 23: An attempted coup d'etat takes place as 200 troops occupy the Spanish parliament; King Juan Carlos refuses to co-operate and the rebels surrender after seven hours.

Prince Charles and Lady Diana announce their engagement on 24 February.

February 1981

Tuesday 24: The existence of the element Bohrium (Bh) is confirmed in Darmstadt, Germany.

The engagement of HRH Prince Charles, Prince of Wales, and Lady Diana Spencer is officially announced from Buckingham Palace.

Wednesday 25: One of the youngest bank robbers in history, a nine year old boy identified only as 'Robert M', steals $118 after holding up a New York bank armed with a .22 calibre pistol. He gives himself up two days later.

Thursday 26: British prime minister Margaret Thatcher and US president Ronald Reagan meet in Washington for talks.

Friday 27: A daring escape takes place at Fleury-Merogis Prison near Paris, France, as convicts Gerard Dupre and Daniel Beaumont flee in a hijacked helicopter. The pair are later apprehended.

Saturday 28: Irish Republican Army (IRA) prisoner Bobby Sands begins a hunger strike in the Maze Prison, Northern Ireland. He dies on 5 May.

Britain's Prime Minister Margaret Thatcher and US President Ronald Reagan meet in Washington.

March 1981

Sunday 1: The musical revue *Sophisticated Ladies*, based on the life of bandleader Duke Ellington, opens in New York City.

Monday 2: The asteroids 4923 Clarke and 5020 Asimov are discovered on the same night by astronomer Schelte J Bus of Hawaii, USA.

Tuesday 3: For the first time, all members of the Soviet Union's ruling Politburo are re-elected to serve five year terms.

Britain's first Homebase DIY superstore opens in Croydon.

Wednesday 4: Britain's Parliament debates the new Sunday football matches, with one MP stating 'the best place to be on Sunday is in church'.

Thursday 5: An attempt to hijack Continental Airlines flight 72 from Los Angeles to Phoenix is foiled when stewards notice a passenger, Victor Malasauskas, is carrying a pistol.

The best-selling Sinclair ZX-81 home computer is launched in the United Kingdom.

Walter Cronkite retires from *CBS News* on 6 March.

March 1981

Left: a typical ZX-81 setup, with TV monitor and cassette tape software drive.

Friday 6: The veteran US newsreader Walter Cronkite makes his final appearance on *CBS Evening News*, which he has presented since 1962.

Saturday 7: Eugenia Charles, Prime Minister of Dominica, announces that a coup plot by former PM Patrick John has been foiled.

Sunday 8: 56 employees at the Tsuruga nuclear power plant in Japan are exposed to radiation following a reactor leak.

Monday 9: The first successful heart-lung transplant is carried out by Dr Bruce Reitz at Stanford University, California.

Tuesday 10: Roger Coleman of Grundy, Virginia, is sentenced to death for the rape and murder of his sister-in-law. He becomes a cause celebre of the anti-death-penalty movement, but after his execution in 1992, DNA proof of his guilt is brought to light.

Wednesday 11: Joseph Sardler, 32, of Mount Airy, North Carolina, blind for five years, finds his sight restored after hitting his head when tripping on his guide dog's water bowl.

March 1981

Thursday 12: Four people are killed when a Sikorsky S-76A helicopter crashes near Peterhead, Aberdeenshire.

Friday 13: The world's first Rubik Cube contest takes place in Munich. The winner is Jury Froschl who solves the puzzle in just 38 seconds.

Saturday 14: A two-week hostage standoff comes to an end as gunmen release 100 passengers held on board a Pakistan Airlines plane at Kabul, Afghanistan.

Sunday 15: Francis Hughes becomes the second IRA prisoner to go on hunger strike in the Maze Prison, Northern Ireland.

Monday 16: A gang of bounty hunters kidnaps the Great Train Robber, Ronnie Biggs, hiding in Brazil since 1963, and attempts to bring him back to Britain to claim the reward for his capture; the attempt fails as Brazil has no extradition treaty with Britain.

Tuesday 17: Italian police begin arrests of members of a secret society known as P2, responsible for embezzling hundreds of millions of dollars from the Ambrosiano Bank.

Phil Mahre (USA) wins the Alpine Ski World Cup on 28 March.

Wednesday 18: The comedy drama series *The Greatest American Hero* starring William Katt is first broadcast on ABC-TV.

Thursday 19: Two ground crew workers are killed by a gas leak during a test of the Space Shuttle *Columbia* at Cape Canaveral.

Friday 20: The supernatural horror film *Omen III: The Final Conflict* starring Sam Neil as the Antichrist is released.

March 1981

Saturday 21: After seven years in the title role, *Dr Who* actor Tom Baker hands over the part to Peter Davison in the episode *Logopolis*.

Left: Dr David Owen, one of the 'Gang of Four' leaders of Britain's newly formed Social Democrat Party, addresses a party meeting.

Sunday 22: Jügderdemidiin Gürragchaa becomes the first Mongolian in space when he travels to the Soviet Salyut 6 space station.

Monday 23: Field Marshal Sir Claude Auchinleck DSO OBE, Commander in Chief of the Indian Army during the Second World War, dies aged 96.

Tuesday 24: West German police carry out raids on the homes of hundreds of suspected neo-Nazis.

Wednesday 25: The largest bank robbery in the history of Sri Lanka takes place as a Tamil separatist gang steals approximately US$400,000 from an armoured car.

Thursday 26: Britain's new Social Democrat Party (SDP) is officially launched in London led by Roy Jenkins and his 'Gang fof Four' defectors from the Labour Party.

Friday 27: A four-hour national strike takes place in communist Poland in support of the Solidarity trade union movement.

March 1981

Saturday 28: Phil Mahre becomes the first American to win the Alpine Ski World Cup held in Switzerland.

Sunday 29: Dick Beardsley (USA) and Inge Simonson (Norway) win the first London Marathon with a joint finish at 2:11:48.

Monday 30: In Washington, DC, President Ronald Reagan is seriously injured when he is shot in the chest at point blank range in an assassination attempt by John Hinckley, Jr. Mr Reagan eventually makes a full recovery.

Tuesday 31: Indonesian commandos rescue all hostages on board the hijacked Garuda Indonesia Flight 206 at Bangkok.

Top left: Ronald Reagan leaves the Washington Hilton Hotel.

Left: moments after he is shot, agents shield the President while two police officers lie injured on the ground.

April 1981

Wednesday 1: NBC and ABC TV in the USA broadcast a recording allegedly made in January of a psychic, Tamara Rand, predicting the shooting of Ronald Reagan. It is later revealed to be a fake, recorded after the assassination attempt.

Thursday 2: Fighting begins again in the Syrian Civil War after a five year ceasefire.

Friday 3: The Osborne 1, the first commercially successful microcomputer, goes on sale in the USA.

Saturday 4: British band Bucks Fizz wins the Eurovision Song Contest with *Making Your Mind Up*.

The Osborne 1.

The Oxford v Cambridge Boat Race is won by Oxford, in the first race to have a female coxswain.

Sunday 5: The 1981 United Kingdom census is conducted.

April 1981

Monday 6: The British novelist Graham Greene is awarded literature's Jerusalem Prize.

Tuesday 7: Large scale manouevres by the armies of the Soviet-allied Warsaw Pact countries are completed, allaying fears in Poland that a military crackdown on trade unions is imminent.

Wednesday 8: General Omar N. Bradley, the US Army's last five-star general of the Second World War, dies aged 88.

Thursday 9: The first case of AIDS (Acquired Immune Deficiency Syndrome) is diagnosed by Dr John Gullett in San Francisco.

Friday 10: The IRA convict Bobby Sands is elected as MP for Fermanagh and South Tyrone while on hunger strike in Northern Ireland's Maze Prison.

Saturday 11: The worst race-riot in Britain's history breaks out in the south London suburb of Brixton. 279 police officers are injured after coming under sustained attack from petrol bombs.

Police with riot shields block Coldharbour Lane in Brixton, South London, during the worst disturbances in the capital for over a century.

April 1981

Sunday 12: 20 years to the day after the Russians sent the first man into space, NASA's reusable Space Shuttle *Columbia* is launched from Cape Canaveral.

The world champion US boxer Joe Louis dies aged 66.

Left: the Space Shuttle *Columbia*.

Monday 13: John Kennedy O'Toole is posthumously awarded the Pulitzer Prize for fiction for *A Confederacy of Dunces*. O'Toole committed suicide in 1969 over his lack of recognition as a writer.

Tuesday 14: The space shuttle *Columbia* returns safely to Earth, despite the loss of some heat-shielding tiles from its bodywork.

Wednesday 15: The *Washington Post* reporter Janet Cooke admits her Pulitzer Prize-winning article on an eight year old heroin addict is a fabrication; she becomes the only winner in the history of the award to return her prize.

Thursday 16: Canadian Prime Minister Pierre Trudeau rejects plans to turn the country into a loose confederation of states.

Friday 17: (Good Friday) 15 people are killed when Air US Flight 716 collides with a parachute training aeroplane over Colorado. Fortunately all but two of the parachutists are able to jump to safety.

April 1981

Saturday 18: The longest professional game in baseball history (8h 25 mins) takes place, between the Pawtucket Red Sox and the Rochester Red Wings at McCoy Stadium, Pawtucket, Rhode Island.

Sunday 19: (Easter Sunday) 15 people are killed in a bomb attack by communist rebels on a church in Davao City in the Phillippines.

Monday 20: In the 85th Boston Marathon Toshihiko Seko of Japan wins the men's race in 2:09:26; Allison Roe of New Zealand takes the women's title in 2:26:46.

The World Snooker Championship is won by 23 year old Steve Davis.

Tuesday 21: The Egyptologist Dorothy Eady, who found fame after claiming to be the reincarnation of an ancient Egyptian priestess 'Omm Sety', dies aged 77.

Wednesday 22: The largest bank robbery in US history to this date takes place in Tucson, Arizona when thieves rob the First National Bank of $3.3m.

Thursday 23: Soviet Politburo representatives meet the Polish government in Warsaw to discuss the growing problem of the Solidarity trade union movement.

Friday 24: US President Ronald Reagan ends the grain embargo to the USSR and calls for talks with Soviet leaders.

The first Monster Truck car-crushing show takes place on 27 April.

April 1981

Saturday 25: The USSR launches the TKS 'space ferry' into orbit.

Sunday 26: The first successful foetal surgery is carried out by Dr Michael R Harrison at the University of California hospital in San Francisco.

Monday 27: The first car-crushing show by a 'monster truck', Bigfoot, takes place in St Louis, Missouri.

The Xerox 8010, the first personal computer to include a mouse, is launched in the USA.

Barbara Bach.

The former Beatle, Ringo Starr, marries the actress Barbara Bach in London.

Tuesday 28: Israel intervenes in the war between Syria and Lebanese Christians for the first time, shooting down two Syrian helicopters.

Wednesday 29: The British serial killer Peter Sutcliffe (the 'Yorkshire Ripper') admits in court to the manslaughter of 13 women on grounds of insanity.

Thursday 30: The low-cost US airline People Express is launched.

May
1981

Friday 1: American Airlines introduces the world's first Frequent Flyer programme.

Saturday 2: The British singer Sheena Easton hits number one in the USA with *Morning Train*.

Sunday 3: The medieval archbishop Symeon of Thessalonica is canonised by the Orthodox Church.

Monday 4: The 40mhz range of the radio spectrum is set aside in the USA for future mobile phone communications.

Tuesday 5: The IRA prisoner Bobby Sands, 27, dies in the Maze Prison, Northern Ireland, after a 66-day hunger strike.

Wednesday 6: Libya's embassy in Washington DC, is ordered to close over terrorism links.

Thursday 7: The standup comedian Jerry Seinfeld performs on TV for the first time, on Johnny Carson's *The Tonight Show*.

Friday 8: The body of Maureen Mosie is discovered in Kamloops, British Columbia. She is believed to be the last of 28 victims of the 'Trans-Canada Highway Killer', who is never caught.

May 1981

Saturday 9: The Football Association (FA) Cup Final at Wembley Stadium, London, ends in a 1-1 draw between Manchester City and Tottenham Hotspur.

Sunday 10: François Mitterrand beats Valéry Giscard d'Estaing in France's Presidential elections.

Monday 11: Andrew Lloyd Webber's hit musical *Cats* opens at the New Theatre, London, for the first of 8,949 performances.

Tuesday 12: Francis Hughes, 25, becomes the second IRA prisoner to die after going on hunger strike in the Maze Prison, Northern Ireland.

François Mitterrand.

Wednesday 13: Pope John Paul II is seriously injured when he is shot in St Peter's, Rome by a Turkish assassin, Mehmet Ali Agca.

Thursday 14: Tottenham Hotspur win the Football Association (FA) Cup in London's Wembley Stadium in a rematch following the draw against Manchester City on 9 May.

Pope John Paul II.

Friday 15: Zara Phillips, second child of HRH Princess Anne and Captain Mark Phillips, is born in London.

The award-winning film *Chariots of Fire*, about Great Britain's 1924 Olympic running team and featuring music by Vangelis, is released in the UK.

Saturday 16: Romania's first cosmonaut, Dumitru Prunariu, goes into space on board the USSR's Soyuz 40 rocket.

May 1981

Sunday 17: The USA's Jeanette Piccard dies aged 86. Mrs Piccard set two notable records: the female altitude record (10 miles in a balloon in 1934) and in 1971 as one of the first eleven women to be ordained as priests in the Episcopalian Church.

Monday 18: Turkish police make two arrests in Istanbul of suspects thought to have assisted Mehmet Ali Agca, who attempted to assassinate the Pope on 13 May.

Tuesday 19: Four policemen of the Royal Ulster Constabulary are killed by a roadside bomb near Bessbrook, County Armagh.

Wednesday 20: A conceptual artist, Lee Waisler, dumps five tons of horse manure outside the offices of the *Los Angeles Times* following a bad review of his works by the paper's art critic. The critic later responds by describing the ordure as 'far more interesting' than Mr Waisler's paintings.

Thursday 21: Following the failure of the film *Heaven's Gate*, United Artists is sold to MGM for $380m.

Friday 22: The British serial killer Peter Sutcliffe, aka the 'Yorkshire Ripper' is sentenced to life imprisonment on 13 counts of murder.

Saturday 23: The first victim of a satanic cult known as the Ripper Crew is found dead in Elmshurst, Illinois. Four other women are murdered before the gang is caught in 1982.

Sunday 24: Jaime Roldós Aguilera, President of Ecuador, is killed in a plane crash.

Monday 25: Daredevil Dan Goodwin is arrested after a 7.5 hour climb to the

Peter Sutcliffe, aka the 'Yorkshire Ripper' is sentenced on 22 May.

May 1981

top of the 1454 feet high Sears Tower in Chicago. Mr Goodwin achieves the feat using rubber suckers, hooks and ropes.

Tuesday 26: Soviet cosmonauts Vladimir Kovalyonok and Viktor Savinykh return to Earth from the *Saluyt 6* space station, after a record 75 days in outer space.

Wednesday 27: Liverpool FC defeats Real Madrid to win soccer's European Cup in Paris, France.

Russian stamp commemorating Vladimir Kovalyonok and Viktor Savinykh.

Thursday 28: Former police officer Laurie 'Bambi' Bembenek murders her husband's ex-wife in Milwaukee, Wisconsin. She achieves nationwide notoriety when she escapes from prison and goes on the run in 1990.

Friday 29: Rosamond Soong Ching-Ling, Vice-President of China, dies aged 88.

Saturday 30: Ziaur Rahman, President of Bangladesh, is assassinated.

Sunday 31: Giuseppe Pella, former prime minister of Italy, dies aged 79.

In county cricket (40 overs), Leicestershire defeats Northamptonshire by 5 wickets; Essex beats Kent on faster scoring.

President Rahman of Bangladesh is assassinated on 30 May.

June 1981

Monday 1: Tests of an anti-missile laser gun by the US Air Force end when the gun fails to bring down a Sidewinder missile travelling at over 2,000 mph over China Lake, California

Tuesday 2: The Ulster loyalist the Reverend Ian Paisley is blamed for leaking the news of an unannounced visit of Princess Alexandra to Belfast to the press.

Wednesday 3: Shergar wins the Epsom Derby.

Thursday 4: James Earl Ray, the assassin of Martin Luther King, survives being stabbed 22 times in an attack by fellow prisoners.

Friday 5: The former Beatle George Harrison releases his album *Somewhere in England*.

George Harrison.

Saturday 6: 800 people are killed when a crowded train crashes in Bihar, India, after attempting to avoid a cow on the tracks.

Sunday 7: In a raid lasting 1 minute 20 seconds, Israeli bomber planes destroy the Osirak nuclear reactor in Iraq.

June 1981

The tennis player Anna Kournikova is born in Moscow, Russia.

Monday 8: A fifth IRA convict, Tom McIlwee, goes on hunger strike in Northern Ireland's Maze Prison.

Tuesday 9: The actress Natalie Portman (*Black Swan*) is born in Jerusalem, Israel.

Wednesday 10: British runner Sebastian Coe sets a world record of 800m in 1 minute 41 seconds, in Florence, Italy, which remains unbeaten until 1997.

Poster for *Raiders of the Lost Ark*.

Thursday 11: Charles Haughey's *Fianna Fáil* party is defeated by Garret FitzGerald's *Fine Gael* coalition in the Republic of Ireland's general election.

Friday 12: The adventure film *Raiders of the Lost Ark* starring Harrison Ford premieres in the USA.

Saturday 13: Marcus Serjeant, 17, fires six shots from a pistol at HM Queen Elizabeth II while she is on horseback at the Trooping the Colour parade in London. The Queen manages to prevent her horse from bolting; it is later revealed the shots were blanks.

Sebastian Coe.

Sunday 14: White and black youths clash in Coventry, England, following a concert by the pop group The Specials.

June 1981

HMS *Ark Royal.*

Monday 15: The US Supreme Court rules in Rhodes v Chapman that making two convicts share a cell designed for one is not 'cruel and unusual punishment'.

Tuesday 16: Ferdinand Marcos is re-elected as President of the Phillippines.

Wednesday 17: The largest submarine to this date, the USS *Ohio*, is launched, costing $1.2 billion.

Thursday 18: The Open Doors missionary society smuggles one million Bibles into China in one night.

Friday 19: The Canadian singer Celine Dion makes her TV debut.

The European Space Agency makes the first successful launch of its *Ariane* rocket.

Saturday 20: The aircraft carrier and Royal Navy flagship HMS *Ark Royal* is launched by HM Queen Elizabeth the Queen Mother.

John McEnroe.

June 1981

Bond girl Carole Bouquet stars in *For Your Eyes Only*.

Sunday 21: Pierre Mauroy becomes Prime Minister of France.

Monday 22: At the Wimbledon tennis championships, US player John McEnroe shouts 'you cannot be serious' in an on-court rant against the umpire.

Tuesday 23: Unemployment in the UK reaches 2.68 million, one in nine of the workforce.

Wednesday 24: The twelfth James Bond film, *For Your Eyes Only* starring Roger Moore and Carole Bouquet is released.

Thursday 25: The US Supreme Court rules in Rostker v Goldberg that women are exempt from military conscription.

Friday 26: The army comedy film *Stripes* starring Bill Murray premieres in the USA.

Saturday 27: The UK's Ministry of Defence orders all copies of a Forestry Commission map to be destroyed after it is found to accidentally have included the location of a secret NATO base near Chepstow, Gwent.

Sunday 28: 74 members of Iran's Islamic Republican Party are killed in a bomb attack on their conference in Tehran.

Monday 29: Hu Yaobang becomes Chairman of the Chinese Communist Party.

Tuesday 30: Israel's general election results in a hung parliament. A coalition under Menachem Begin is eventually established.

July 1981

Wednesday 1: 150 people are killed as Typhoon Kelly hits the Phillipines.

Thursday 2: The US Supreme Court rules that the former President Carter acted lawfully in returning seized Iranian assets in exchange for the release of 52 US hostages.

Friday 3: Chris Evert Lloyd wins the ladies' singles tennis championships at Wimbledon.

Saturday 4: John McEnroe wins the mens' singles tennis championships at Wimbledon.

Sunday 5: Rajan Mahadevan of Mangalore, India, sets a world record by reciting Pi to 31,811 places from memory.

Monday 6: While under cross-examination in a Los Angeles court, the 'Hillside Strangler' suspect Kenneth Bianchi unexpectedly makes

Chris Evert Lloyd.

July 1981

The Solar Challenger plane in flight.

The Donkey Kong arcade game.

a full confession to a string of murders of young women in the 1970s.

Tuesday 7: Sandra Day O'Connor becomes the first woman to serve on the US Supreme Court.

Stephen Ptacek makes the first crossing of the English Channel in a solar-powered plane, the *Solar Challenger*.

Wednesday 8: The IRA member Joe McDonnell dies in Long Kesh internment camp in Northern Ireland after a 61 day hunger strike.

British Leyland ends production of the Austin Maxi family car after 12 years.

Thursday 9: Nintendo launches the *Donkey Kong* video game.

Friday 10: A 'town bully', Kevin Rex McElroy, is shot dead in front of a crowd in Skidmore, Missouri, after a decades-long reign of terror in the town. Despite there being at least 46 witnesses to his killing, nobody is ever identified as the culprit.

July 1981

Saturday 11: Race riots break out in cities across the UK, with major disturbances in London, Birmingham and Manchester.

Sunday 12: 1.5 million people are made homeless after China's Yangtze River floods after 18.8 inches (480mm) of rain in three days.

Monday 13: Martin Hurson becomes the sixth IRA hunger striker to die.

Tuesday 14: Max Hugel, chief of clandestine operations at the CIA, resigns over allegations of fraudulent stock trading.

Wednesday 15: The artificial sweetener aspartame, marketed as NutraSweet, goes on sale in the USA.

Thursday 16: The folk singer Harry Chapin is killed in a car accident on the Long Island Expressway, New York.

Friday 17: 114 people are killed when an overhead walkway collapses in the Hyatt Regency Hotel, Kansas City, Missouri.

HM Queen Elizabeth II opens the Humber Bridge in north east England. It is the world's longest suspension bridge to this date.

England's Humber Bridge, the world's longest suspension bridge at this date, opens on 17 July.

July 1981

The collapsed walkway of the Hyatt Regency.

Saturday 18: A convicted murderer turned novelist, Jack Abbott, is himself murdered following an argument with a fellow diner in a New York cafe, while on parole promoting his book, *In the Belly of the Beast*.

Sunday 19: Following revelations that the Soviets have been stealing technical secrets, the US government creates faulty software and allows it to be stolen, causing the USSR's Siberian gas pipeline to fail.

Monday 20: The Czechoslovakian tennis star, Martina Navratilova, becomes a US citizen.

Tuesday 21: Tohui, the first panda to be born and survive in captivity outside China, is born in Mexico City.

Wednesday 22: Mehmet Ali Agca is sentenced to life imprisonment for his attempt to kill the Pope on 13 May.

Thursday 23: A coal mine fire burning since 1962 breaks to the surface in the town of Centralia, Pennsylvania. The town is later abandoned.

Friday 24: The Lebanese Civil War is temporarily halted when American negotiator Philip Habib brokers a ceasefire between Israel and the PLO.

US Special Envoy Philip Habib.

July 1981

Saturday 25: The first World Games, the international competition for non-Olympic sports, is held in Santa Clara, California.

Sunday 26: The FBI's six year long undercover infiltration of the Mafia comes to an end. The operation inspires the 1997 film *Donnie Brasco* starring Al Pacino and Johnny Depp.

Monday 27: US President Ronald Reagan announces the largest tax cut in American history with his Economic Recovery Tax Act.

British Telecom becomes an independent entity separate from the Royal Mail.

Tuesday 28: A 7.3 magnitude earthquake hits the Kerman province of Iran.

Wednesday 29: The wedding of HRH Prince Charles, Prince of Wales, and Lady Diana Spencer takes place at London's St Paul's Cathedral. It is watched on television by an estimated 750 million people worldwide.

Thursday 30: A coup takes place in The Gambia while the country's president, Dawda Jawara, is away attending the Royal Wedding in London.

Friday 31: A six week long major league baseball players' strike in the USA comes to an end.

Sir Dawda Jawara.

July 1981

**Their Royal Highnesses
the Prince and Princess of Wales
on their wedding day, 29 July 1981.**

August 1981

Saturday 1: The Music Television Cable Network (MTV) goes on the air in the USA. The first song played is *Video Killed the Radio Star* by The Buggles.

Sunday 2: Mohammed Ali Rajai becomes President of Iran.

Monday 3: US air traffic controllers go on strike.

Tuesday 4: The Hollywood star Melvyn Douglas dies aged 80.

Wednesday 5: US President Ronald Reagan orders the dismissal of 11,359 striking air traffic controllers under a law forbidding strikes by federal employees.

Left: British band The Buggles are the first to appear on MTV.
Above: The MTV logo.

August 1981

The IBM computer with Windows MS-DOS is launched on 12 August.

Thursday 6: Production of the neutron bomb, the atomic weapon which kills personnel but leaves buildings and equipment intact, begins in the USA.

Friday 7: The *Washington Star* newspaper ceases publication after 128 years.

Saturday 8: The tennis champion Roger Federer is born in Bottmingen, Switzerland.

Sunday 9: Golfer Larry Nelson wins the PGA Championship in Duluth, Georgia.

Monday 10: British TV ratings reveal the wedding of Prince Charles and Princess Diana was watched by 1.5 million fewer people than the wedding of the fictional characters Ken Barlow and Deirdre Langton on the soap opera *Coronation Street*.

Roger Federer is born on 8 August.

Tuesday 11: Canadian air traffic controllers end a two day boycott of US flights in sympathy with the dismissal of over 11,000 striking American controllers on 5 August.

Wednesday 12: The IBM personal computer, featuring Microsoft's MS-DOS software, is launched in the USA.

August 1981

Thursday 13: Queen Beatrix of the Netherlands moves her official residence from Soestdijk Palace near Utrecht to Ten Bosch Palace in the Hague.

Friday 14: The 1980s revival of 3D films begins with the release of the western drama *Comin'at Ya* starring Tony Anthony and Victoria Abril.

Saturday 15: English cricketer Ian Botham scores a record 100 runs for 86 balls against Australia in the Fifth Test at Old Trafford.

Sunday 16: A major international child-selling ring is broken up in Bogota, Colombia, which had arranged falsified adoptions for wealthy foreigners.

Monday 17: The British government opens an inquiry into the recent riots in Moss Side, Manchester.

Tuesday 18: The first commercial 'vaping' device is patented in the USA. A tube impregnated with nicotine, the product is later marketed as 'Favor Tobacco Free Cigarettes'.

The first smokeless cigarettes are patented on 18 August.

Wednesday 19: A dogfight takes place between USAF and Libyan jets over the Gulf of Sidra; it is the first engagement of US aircraft since 1973.

Thursday 20: Michael Devine, 27, becomes the tenth and last of the IRA hunger strikers to die.

Friday 21: The comedy horror film *An American Werewolf in London* starring David Naughton and Jenny Agutter premieres in the UK.

August 1981

Saturday 22: 110 people are killed when Far Eastern Air Transport flight 103 explodes over Taiwan, probably due to corrosion in the hold.

Sunday 23: 40 people are killed and 20,000 people are left homeless when Typhoon Thad hits Japan.

Monday 24: The first electronic camera, the Mavica, is launched by Sony. It is not a digital camera, but works by capturing still video images on a floppy disk.

Saturn photographed by *Voyager 2*.

Tuesday 25: The space probe *Voyager 2* makes its closest approach to Saturn, passing within 26,000 miles of the ringed planet.

Wednesday 26: General Motors launches the Vauxhall Cavalier MkII in the UK. (Marketed as the Chevrolet Cavalier in the USA).

Thursday 27: A USAF spyplane flying in South Korean airspace escapes unharmed when it it attacked with a North Korean surface to air missile.

The Sony Mavica, the world's first electronic camera, is launched on 24 August.

Friday 28: Britain's Sebastian Coe sets the world record for running a mile at 3.46.32 in Brussels, Belgium.

August 1981

Saturday 29: Two people are killed when Palestinian Abu Nidal terrorists attack a synagogue in Vienna, Austria.

Sunday 30: Iran's Prime Minister Bahonar and President Raja'I are assassinated in Tehran by Mujahadeen terrorists.

Monday 31: The first satellite radio broadcasting service begins in the USA, enabling local radio to be broadcast from a centralised location.

The Vauxhall Cavalier MkII is launched in the UK on 26 August. In the USA it is badged as the Chevrolet Cavalier.

September 1981

Tuesday 1: The Nazi Party's chief architect Albert Speer dies aged 81.

As petrol (gasoline) prices reach £1 per gallon in the UK, fuel begins to be sold by the litre rather than the gallon in order to retain pumps with a maximum calibration of 99.9p per gallon.

Wednesday 2: The German film *Marianne and Juliane* wins the Golden Lion award at the 38th Venice International Film Festival.

Thursday 3: 1536 Islamic activists are arrested in Egypt in a clampdown by the Prime Minister, Anwar Sadat.

Friday 4: King Sobhuza II of Swaziland becomes the first monarch since Queen Victoria to celebrate a Diamond Jubilee.

The singer Beyoncé Knowles is born in Houston, Texas.

Saturday 5: The English football player John Barnes makes his professional debut for Watford FC, aged 17.

Beyoncé Knowles is born on 4 September.

September 1981

Former US President Ford shows President and Mrs Ronald Reagan around the Gerald R Ford Museum on 17 September.

Sunday 6: One person is killed and several injured in a major explosion which destroys the Chemstar chemical factory at Stalybridge, Manchester, England.

Monday 7: *The People's Court,* the first legal reality TV show, is first broadcast on US TV.

Tuesday 8: The first episode of the long running sitcom *Only Fools and Horses* is broadcast on BBC TV.

Wednesday 9: The French psychoanalyst Jacques Lacan dies aged 80.

Thursday 10: Picasso's epic painting of the Spanish Civil War, *Guernica*, is returned to the Prado gallery in Madrid after being held for safekeeping in New York since 1939.

Friday 11: One of the USA's premier music venues, the Swing Auditorium in San Bernadino, California, is irreparably damaged when a Cessna light aircraft crashes into it.

Saturday 12: The cartoon series *The Smurfs* is first broadcast on NBC TV.

September 1981

Sunday 13: Kare Willoch becomes Prime Minister of Norway.

Monday 14: Panic buying begins in the USSR as major price hikes on many essential goods are announced; motor fuel prices increase by 100%.

Tuesday 15: A failed assassination attempt is made on General Frederick J Kroesen, commander of the US Army in Europe.

Wednesday 16: The stop-motion animation series *Postman Pat* is first broadcast on BBC TV.

Thursday 17: The Gerald R Ford Presidential Museum opens in Grand Rapids, Michigan.

Friday 18: British politician David Steel famously tells the members of the SDP-Liberal Alliance to 'go back to your constituencies and prepare for government'. The party does not achieve that goal for 29 years, and then only as a coalition.

Saturday 19: Singers Simon and Garfunkel reunite to perform a free concert in New York's Central Park, attended by almost half a million people.

Simon and Garfunkel.

September 1981

Sunday 20: China launches its first three satellites into orbit.

Monday 21: The former colony of Belize (British Honduras) becomes independent of the UK.

Tuesday 22: The US home improvement chain store Home Depot is floated on the stock exchange.

Wednesday 23: The US government announces it will set up a radio station, Radio Marti, for communist Cuba.

Thursday 24: Ford UK announces the end of production of its Cortina saloon car, in production since 1962, and its replacement by the Sierra.

The Rolling Stones on their US tour.

Friday 25: The Rolling Stones begin their 40-city 'Tattoo You' tour of the USA with a concert in JFK Stadium, Philadelphia.

Saturday 26: The Boeing 767 jet air liner makes its first flight.

Tennis star Serena Williams is born in Saginaw, Michigan.

Sunday 27: France's high speed TGV train service between Paris and Lyons goes into operation, travelling at speeds of up to 156mph.

Monday 28: 'Blue Monday': large falls take place in stock markets all over the world, with record drops on the Tokyo Nikkei 225 and London's FT Index.

September 1981

Ford Motors announces the end of the long-running Cortina saloon car on 24 September.

Tuesday 29: US President Reagan issues an executive order to halt the flow of migrants from Haiti.

Bill Shankly, the legendary manager of football team Liverpool FC dies aged 68.

Wednesday 30: The International Olympic Committee awards the 1988 Winter Olympics to Calgary and the Summer Olympics to Seoul, Korea.

The French TGV train begins the Paris to Lyons route on 27 September.

October 1981

Thursday 1: The world's first cellular telephone system goes into operation in Sweden.

Friday 2: The Ayatollah Ali Khamenei becomes President of Iran.

Saturday 3: The seven-month hunger strike by IRA prisoners in Northern Ireland is called off after ten prisoners die.

Sunday 4: The body of Lee Harvey Oswald, the assassin of John F Kennedy, is exhumed to quell suspicions that Oswald was actually a Soviet imposter.

Monday 5: Depeche Mode release their first album, *Speak and Spell*.

The last Triumph sports car, the TR7, is produced in England.

Tuesday 6: Anwar Sadat, President of Egypt, is assassinated.

Wednesday 7: British Leyland launches the Triumph Acclaim small saloon car.

The new Triumph Acclaim.

October 1981

Thursday 8: The pilot episode of the crime series *Cagney and Lacey* is broadcast in the USA.

Friday 9: The death penalty is abolished in France.

Saturday 10: Two people are killed in an IRA bomb attack on London's Chelsea Barracks.

Sunday 11: John Shoecroft and Fred Gorrell make the first non-stop transcontinental balloon flight in the USA in *Super Chicken III*.

Monday 12: The classic drama series *Brideshead Revisited*, starring Anthony Andrews and Jeremy Irons, is first broadcast on British television.

Anthony Andrews, star of *Brideshead Revisited*.

Tuesday 13: Hosni Mubarak, provisional leader of Egypt following Anwar Sadat's assassination, is installed as President after an emergency referendum.

Wednesday 14: The Republic of Ireland defeats France 3-2 in the Rugby World Cup qualifier at Lansdowne Road, Dublin.

Thursday 15: British politician Norman Tebbit makes his famous speech in Parliament of how his father in the 1930s 'got on his bike and looked for work'. The press misquotes it as an insult to the unemployed, 'on your bike!'

Left: Anwar Sadat, the Egyptian President assassinated on 6 October.

October 1981

Moshe Dayan dies on 16 October.

Andreas Papandreou.

Friday 16: The Israeli general and politician Moshe Dayan, famous for his distinctive eyepatch, dies aged 66.

Saturday 17: Pope John Paul II meets with Abuna Takla Haymanot, leader of the Ethiopian Orthodox Church, for ecumenical talks.

Sunday 18: Andreas Papandreou is elected Prime Minister of Greece.

Monday 19: British Telecom announces that its telegram service, in use for 139 years, will be withdrawn in 1982.

Tuesday 20: Far-left radicals attack a Brinks' armoured car in Nanuet, New York, killing a guard and two police officers and stealing $1.7m.

Wednesday 21: A US patent is granted for Caller ID, invented by Joseph O'Neil, Thomas Quinn and Tse Lin Wang.

Thursday 22: The International Meeting on Co-Operation and Development (the North-South Summit) takes place in Cancun, Mexico.

Friday 23: The national debt of the USA passes one trillion dollars.

Saturday 24: Anti-nuclear demonstrations take place in cities across Europe, in protest against the siting of American Pershing missiles in five countries.

October 1981

Sunday 25: The twelfth New York City marathon is won by Alberto Salazar (2:08:13) and Allison Roe (2:25:29).

Monday 26: Rock group Queen releases their *Greatest Hits* album. It goes on to become the all time best selling album in Britain.

HOME TAPING IS KILLING MUSIC
AND IT'S ILLEGAL

The BPI campaign logo.

Tuesday 27: The British Phonographic Industry (BPI) begins a campaign against domestic taping of records, with the slogan 'Home Taping is Killing Music'.

Wednesday 28: In baseball, the Los Angeles Dodgers win the 1981 World Series.

The heavy metal band Metallica is formed in Los Angeles.

Thursday 29: The situation comedy *Gimme A Break!* is first broadcast in the USA.

Friday 30: The Venera 13 probe is launched in the USSR; it lands on Venus in March 1982.

Saturday 31: American explorer Tom Crotser claims to have discovered the biblical Ark of the Covenant in a cave in Lebanon; its authenticity is dismissed upon examination by archaeologists.

Freddie Mercury of Queen.

November 1981

Sunday 1: The West Indian colony of Antigua and Barbuda becomes independent of Britain, in a handover ceremony attended by HRH Princess Margaret.

Monday 2: A Poseidon nuclear missile is dropped 17 feet while being loaded on board the USS *Holland* at Holy Loch, Scotland; the area is evacuated but no damage is sustained.

Tuesday 3: Residents of the island of Barbuda demonstrate for separation from neighouring Antigua following the two islands' independence from Britain on 1 November.

Wednesday 4: The second launch of the Space Shuttle Columbia is called off 31 seconds before lift-off following a technical failure.

Thursday 5: It is announced from Buckingham Palace that HRH Princess Diana is pregnant. HRH Prince William, heir to the British throne, is born on 21 June 1982.

Friday 6: British Prime Minister Margaret Thatcher and the Prime Minister of the Republic of Ireland, Garret Fitzgerald, hold talks on the formation of the Anglo-Irish Intergovernmental Council.

November 1981

Saturday 7: The skeleton of St Lucy, martyred in 304 AD, is stolen from the church of San Geremia in Venice. The remains are recovered by police on 13 December.

Sunday 8: Mark Eyskens is forced out of office as Prime Minister of Belgium after only eight months.

Monday 9: Slavery is abolished in Mauritania following a UN human rights commission.

Tuesday 10: The Chinese government formally criticises the US government for its arms sales to Taiwan.

Wednesday 11: The largest submarine to this date, the USS *Ohio*, is commissioned.

Thursday 12: The Space Shuttle Columbia goes on its second mission, becoming the first spacecraft to be re-used.

Double Eagle V becomes the first balloon to cross the Pacific Ocean.

US President Ronald Reagan speaks to the crew of *Columbia* from Mission Control, Houston.

November 1981

Astronaut Story Musgrave attached to the Canadarm robot arm system in space.

Friday 13: The Canadian-built robotic arm system known as the Canadarm is used for the first time in space from the Columbia shuttle.

Saturday 14: A Northern Ireland member of Parliament, the Reverend Robert Bradford, an outspoken critic of the IRA, is assassinated in Belfast.

Sunday 15: Abdus Sattar becomes President of Bangladesh.

Monday 16: The highest ever audience for a US daytime soap opera is achieved when 14 million households tune in to *General Hospital* to watch the wedding of Luke Spencer and Laura Webber.

Tuesday 17: US President Reagan takes the decision to support the Contras rebel force in opposition to the socialist regime in Nicaragua.

Wednesday 18: The English national football team beats Hungary 1-0 at Wembley Stadium to qualify for the 1982 World Cup.

Thursday 19: The African National Congress campaigner Griffiths Mxenge is assassinated by South African secret police.

November 1981

Friday 20: US Steel agrees to pay $6.3 billion for a takeover of Marathon Oil.

Saturday 21: The tanker Globe Asimi spills 16,000 tons of fuel oil in the Baltic Sea off the coast of Lithuania.

Sunday 22: Pope John Paul II publishes the exhortation *Familiaris Consortio* on the role of the Christian family in the modern world.

Robert Mulddoon becomes Prime Minister of New Zealand on 28 November.

Monday 23: The largest tornado outbreak in European history takes place as 104 tornados touch down across Wales and England, causing damage to hundreds of properties.

Tuesday 24: Over 600 people are killed when Typhoon Irma hits the Philippines.

Wednesday 25: A group of mercenaries led by the ex-British army gun-for-hire 'Mad Mike' Hoare attempts a failed military coup in the Seychelles.

Thursday 26: The Spanish senate votes to join NATO.

Friday 27: Bones said to be those of Buddha are discovered in a cave near Peking (Beijing), China.

The Austrian singer and actress Lotte Lenya dies aged 83.

Singer Lotte Lenya dies on 27 November.

Saturday 28: Robert Muldoon becomes Prime Minister of New Zealand.

November 1981

Sunday 29: The actress Natalie Wood, ex-wife of actor Robert Wagner, drowns in suspicious circumstances off the coast of southern California. A coroner's report rules it an accident.

Monday 30: Arms reduction talks begin between the USA and USSR in Geneva.

Actress Natalie Wood dies in suspicious circumstances on 29 November.

December 1981

Tuesday 1: 180 people are killed when a Yugoslavian tourist jet crashes in Corsica.

Wednesday 2: The singer Britney Spears is born in McComb, Mississippi.

Thursday 3: Walter Knott, creator of the first US theme park, Knott's Berry Farm, dies aged 91.

Friday 4: The longest jail sentence on record is handed out, as triple murderer Dudley Wayne Kyzer is sent to prison for 10,000 years in Alabama.

Singer Britney Spears is born on 2 December.

Saturday 5: 11 of the 12 members of the Hawaiian skydiving team are killed when their plane goes out of control near Pearl Harbor; one member manages to parachute to safety.

Sunday 6: In an interview with ABC TV, Libya's President Gaddafi denies rumours that he has ordered the assassination of President Reagan.

December 1981

Monday 7: Manufacture of Lockheed's new L101 *TriStar* jumbo jet is cancelled due to a low number of orders.

Tuesday 8: Arthur Scargill becomes President of Britain's National Union of Mineworkers (NUM).

Severe snowstorms hit Britain, with the lowest temperatures recorded in over a century.

Wednesday 9: The British government announces a £95m aid package for the inner cities in response to recent rioting.

Thursday 10: Javier Perez de Cuellar becomes Secretary General of the United Nations; Spain joins NATO.

Friday 11: Four people are killed in a train crash during a severe blizzard at Seer, Buckinghamshire.

Muhammed Ali, 39, is defeated by Trevor Berbick in his last professional boxing match.

Saturday 12: The first case of AIDS is diagnosed in the UK.

The deposed Queen Camphoui of Laos, 69, dies in a communist gulag at Sop Hao.

Soviet T-25 tanks patrol the streets of Warsaw as martial law is declared in Poland.

December 1981

Sunday 13: In Poland, martial law is declared at 6.00 am and all private telephones cut off in a clampdown on the trade union Solidarity.

Temperatures fall to a record low in England, with -25.2C/-13.4F recorded in Shrewsbury, Shropshire.

Monday 14: The Golan Heights region of Syria is offically annexed to Israel.

Tuesday 15: The government of Argentina begins plans for its 1982 invasion of Britain's Falkland Islands.

Wednesday 16: 13 people are killed as police and troops break up a coal miners' strike in Wujek, Poland.

Thursday 17: Brigadier James L Dozier, US Army, is kidnapped by Red Brigade terrorists in Italy. He is eventually freed on 28 January 1982.

Friday 18: Robert Patlescu, aged 19 months, survives a fall from a sixth storey window in Manhattan without injury.

Brigadier Dozier is kidnapped on 17 December.

Saturday 19: 16 people including eight lifeboat volunteers are killed off the coast of Penlee in Cornwall, south west England, in the worst British sea disaster since 1946.

Sunday 20: The musical *Dreamgirls* premieres on Broadway. It goes on to win six Tony Awards and runs for 1521 performances.

Monday 21: The Common Market for Eastern and Southern Africa (COMESA) is set up.

December 1981

Tuesday 22: The Corporate Angel Network programme is set up in the USA, offering empty airline seats to hospital patients requiring transport.

Wednesday 23: US President Ronald Reagan announces sanctions on Poland following its declaration of martial law.

Thursday 24: In a televised address, US President Ronald Reagan urges Americans to display Christmas Eve candles in solidarity with the people of Poland suffering under martial law.

Jazz legend Hoagy Carmichael dies on 27 December.

Friday 25: Leonid Brezhnev, leader of the USSR, condemns US President Ronald Reagan's stance on Poland, calling it 'interference in the internal affairs of a sovereign state'.

Pope John Paul II appeals for religious freedom in Soviet countries in his Christmas Day sermon.

Saturday 26: A US doctor, Robert Abrams, announces his invention of a 'bedside computer'whic h will monitor a woman's fertility levels to facilitate natural family planning.

Sunday 27: Australian cricketer Dennis Lillee sets the record for career Test wickets, reaching 310 during the second Test against the West Indies in Melbourne.

Jazz pianist Hoagy Carmichael dies aged 82.

Soviet leader Leonid Brezhnev.

December 1981

Stevie Wonder.

Monday 28: Elizabeth Jordan Carr becomes the first 'test tube baby' to be born in the USA.

Tuesday 29: US President Ronald Reagan extends sanctions against the USSR over its support for martial law in Poland.

Wednesday 30: Singer Stevie Wonder releases his hit single, *That Girl.*

Thursday 31: Flight Lieutenant Jerry Rawlings seizes power in a military coup in Ghana.

Other titles from Montpelier Publishing:

A Little Book of Limericks: Funny Rhymes for all the Family
ISBN 9781511524124

Scottish Jokes: A Wee Book of Clean Caledonian Chuckles
ISBN 9781495297366

The Old Fashioned Joke Book: Gags and Funny Stories
ISBN 9781514261989

Non-Religious Funeral Readings: Philosophy and Poetry for Secular Services
ISBN 9781500512835

Large Print Jokes: Hundreds of Gags in Easy-to-Read Type
ISBN 9781517775780

Spiritual Readings for Funerals and Memorial Services
ISBN 9781503379329

Victorian Murder: True Crimes, Confessions and Executions
ISBN 9781530296194

Large Print Prayers: A Prayer for Each Day of the Month
ISBN 9781523251476

A Little Book of Ripping Riddles and Confounding Conundrums
ISBN 9781505548136

Vinegar uses: over 150 ways to use vinegar
ISBN 9781512136623

Large Print Wordsearch: 100 Puzzles in Easy-to-Read Type
ISBN 9781517638894

The Pipe Smoker's Companion
ISBN 9781500441401

The Book of Church Jokes
ISBN 9781507620632

Bar Mitzvah Notebook
ISBN 9781976007781

Jewish Jokes
ISBN 9781514845769

Large Print Address Book
ISBN 9781539820031

How to Cook Without a Kitchen: Easy, Healthy and Low-Cost Meals
9781515340188

Large Print Birthday Book
ISBN 9781544670720

Retirement Jokes
ISBN 9781519206350

Take my Wife: Hilarious Jokes of Love and Marriage
ISBN 9781511790956

Welsh Jokes: A Little Book of Wonderful Welsh Wit
ISBN 9781511612241

1001 Ways to Save Money: Thrifty Tips for the Fabulously Frugal!
ISBN 9781505432534

Available online at Amazon.com

Printed in Great Britain
by Amazon